THE

FIRE AND HAMMER

OF

GOD'S WORD

AGAINST THE

SIN OF SLAVERY.

SPEECH OF

GEORGE B. CHEEVER, D. D.,

AT THE ANNIVERSARY OF THE AMERICAN ABOLITION SOCIETY, MAY, 1858.

PRICES OF DR. CHEEVER'S SPEECH.

UNCOVERED—2 cents per single copy.
20 cents per dozen.
$1.50 per hundred.

IN TRACT FORM—Same prices.

COVERED—3 cents per single copy.
30 cents per dozen.
$2.25 per hundred.

POSTAGE—for either kind, 1 cent each.

SPEECH.

Mr. President: We are driven this day to God. Apart from his word, and his grace to make his word effectual, and to keep it even in the hearts of his children from perversion, there is no hope in the heart of any political party, nor any Christian party, for the poor slave. We have seen, that men of professed piety, men of age, gray hairs, experience, eloquence, can plead the very authority of the word of God for concealing and denying that word; can call upon Christ to bear witness that their first Christian duty is to take down his light from the candlestick and to put it under a bushel; can deliberately in the name of God, so pervert the salt of Christian truth, as to make it nothing but an additional corrupting element on the dunghill of the world's corruptions. We have seen an eloquent Bishop, with silver locks, pleading for silence on the sin of Slavery, and justifying the Executive Committee of the Tract Society, as possessing an indestructible negative against the instructions of their constituents, and in opposition to the will and word of God, by virtue of being the managers of a great Circumlocution Office, the perfection of whose sagacity and strength is in the art, *How not to do it.* We can not but remember the answer of God, "To him that knoweth to do good, and doeth it not, to him it is sin;" and the judgment of the Lord Jesus: "Inasmuch as ye did it not to one of the least of these my brethren, ye did it not to me."

We have also seen venerable and Christian men not shrinking to denounce the declaration that American Slavery is sin, as *ultra* and inexpedient, and exposing the cause of righteousness to defeat and ruin. Paul rejoiced, in his day, that he had not shunned to declare the whole counsel of God. The professed followers of Paul in our day, do not shun to rebuke such declaration as fanatical and rash. Before such developments, were it not that our trust is in God and not man, we should have no more any strength, or life, or courage left in us. There is no hope, apart from God's word, and from the full and faithful application of it. There is wanting the element of conscientious, stubborn, heart-felt, eternal hostility against Slavery as sin, as reprobated and forbidden of God in the same catalogue with lying, perjury, murder, whoremongering, piracy, man-stealing, and guilt, that, by the law not of God only, but man, is worthy of death. Where shall such an element be found? How shall it be created, quickened, trained? Not in the school of political self-seeking and expediency; not under obedience to fugitive-slave laws; not under proclamations and assertions of allegiance to Dred Scott decisions; not in the school of unrighteous and oppressive statutes; not under the law of silence on the word of God—silence in the pulpit—silence in the Tract House; but under the law of fire and thunder in the manifestation of the truth to every man's conscience in the sight of God—by revealing the wrath of God from heaven against all unrighteousness and ungodliness of men, and against this stupendous iniquity as foremost and most germinating in enormity and malignity, most sweeping and accumulating in the habits and materials of sin and misery, the elements and securities of national ruin. Our only hope is in the revived, living, faithful religion of a free, out-spoken, consistent Church, and a fearless, unmuzzled, faithful ministry. Our only hope is in a conscience fastened to the word of God, and a heart flaming with its sacred fire; a popular Church and ministry, holding forth the word of life, and giving themselves up to its supremacy, in such an unrestricted abandonment of all things to its sovereignty, (not the popular sovereignty, but God's sovereignty,) that it may have free course, and be glorified.

The intensity of the plague with us, the exasperation and strength of the iniquity and the evil, are in the provisions for its perpetuity and the insurances of its increase. Not content with enduring it ourselves, for one generation, we have by law entailed it upon others; and the generations to come, as God distributes the consequences, must inevitably rise up and call each preceding generation accursed. If this sin had a possible death, like that of intemperance in the grave of the present drunkard, and were not propagated by a legal fatalism forbidding it to die out, or to be renounced, or the will to be broken—a legal fatalism and missionary zeal united, providing future victims for it in the fastest ratio of increase in human population—then would the evil be comparatively trifling, and the sin would speedily come to an end. But there is no such limit, no such natural consumption or wearing out, no such release by death; the evil and the sin are carefully secured *against* death, and injected, as the heart's blood, into the veins of the next generation, and any attempt to stop the process, throws the whole system into convulsions.

We practise the iniquity upon children, innocent children, the natives of our own land, unbought, unsold, unpaid for, without consultation or consent of father or mother, or the shadow of a permission from the Almighty; and they, the new-born babes of this system, are the compound interest year by year added to the sin and its capital, which thus doubles upon us in the next generation, and must treble in another. We make use of the most sacred domestic affections, of maternal, filial, and, I was going to say, connubial love—but the system forbids, and I have to say *contubernal*—for such rapid and accumulating production of the iniquity, as shall be in some measure adequate to the demand. The whole family relation, the whole domestic state, is prostituted, poisoned, turned into a misery-making machine for the agent of all evil. What God meant should be the source and inspiration of happiness, becomes the fountain of sin and woe. The sacred names of husband, wife, father, mother, son, daughter, babe, become the exponents of various forces and values in the slave-breeding institute. And the whole perfection, completeness, and concentration of this creative power in this manufacturing interest, descends like a trip-hammer on the children, beating them from the birth into marketable articles, and stamping and sealing them as chattels, foredoomed and fatalized to run till they wear out, as living spindles, wheels, activities of labor and productiveness in the same horrible system.

And each generation of immortal marketable stuff is as exactly fashioned in these grooves, moulds, channels, wefted, netted, and drawn through, to come out the invariable product, as the yards of carpeting are cut from the loom to be trodden on, or as the coins drop from the die for the circulation of society. This is the peculiarity of the sin of Slavery in the foremost Christian country on the face of the earth. In this branch of native industry and manufacture we are self-reliant. Disavowing a protective policy in almost every thing else, we are proudly patriotic for the security, superiority, and abundance of this most sacred native product of domestic manufacture, and for neither the raw material nor the bleaching of it, will we depend on any other country in the world.

This is the manner, these are the principles, on which we obey the precepts and fulfill the glories of the 72d Psalm. Instead of obeying God in delivering the children of the needy from deceit and violence, we foredoom them to all the oppression endured by their fathers; instead of judging the poor with righteousness, and the children of the oppressed with equity, we deliberately and solemnly give them over to oppression, as incapable of brotherhood and citizenship, and having no rights that white men are bound to respect. Instead of removing every yoke, we predestinate them *for* the yoke, and perpetuate the yoke for *them*, as a fixture prepared from the birth—the controlling, governing, supreme domestic law—the guiding institution and policy of the house, the State, the nation.

By thus laying our grasp on an unborn race; by saying beforehand to immortal beings, the work of the Creator, You can not come into God's world but as infant slaves, articles of property and merchandise, but with a curse of our national justice and equity branding you for the slave-pen, and separating you from the manhood of all mankind; by this robbery from God and man we become a nation of men-stealers —a community of baptized Thugs for the kidnapping of the children of four millions of people, and the assassination of their personality.

If this were done now, for the first time, to a nation by themselves; if we made a descent upon Africa, China, India, or elsewhere, and carried off into hopeless slavery the children of four millions, the universe would utter a roar of terror and indignation at such a crime. But organize it into a system—make this robbery and moral assassination a fixture of law and policy from generation to generation, and set up its support as the watchword of a powerful political party, the test of faithfulness and patriotism, and the security of an unlimited command of the whole patronage of the United States Government, and forthwith the sanction and sustaining of it become the shining virtue of compromise and expediency, and he is the dangerous man and the mad-man in the community who undertakes to disturb this arrangement, or to agitate the conscience in regard to it. Forthwith, it is no longer the sin which is regarded with astonishment and horror, but the denunciation of it as sin! It is no longer the perpetrators of such a crime, and its supporters, who are to be the objects of reproach and condemnation, but those who cause the truth to burn against the crime —those who call it by the name with which God has branded it, and visit it with the reprobation that God has laid upon it.

And especially the political world and the Pharisees of political Churches stand in horror of the very bad spirit, the unchristian spirit, of those who denounce this wickedness with the direct application of the word of God. It is a subject which must be excluded from the pulpit, because it is a sin enthroned in state, a political sin, to be treated only by political quacks, with political drenches, platforms, cataplasms, and compromises, which the only duty of the Church and the ministry is quietly to indorse and sanction, for the sake of peace.

The system of Slavery is now at length asserted to be the chosen missionary institute of the Lord Almighty. And, admitting it to be such, we are certainly foremost of all the nations in carrying forward the great missionary work. If the appointed work to be done for the children of the needy is that of branding and training them as chattels and brute beasts for the market, we have no rivals in this honor. This is, in fact, the greatest, vastest, most persevering missionary work that we perform. Our instrumentality in binding down in hopeless bondage the children of four millions of immortal beings, guilty of a skin not colored like our own, is our largest instrumentality, thus far, in the glories of the millenium.

By our laws providing that the slave and its increase shall be deemed and doomed our personal chattels forever, we constitute for them a millennium of sin and misery. We convert them into a community, in which it is impossible that the fundamental laws of Christianity should be recognized and obeyed, or the most commonly acknowledged and most sacred institutions of the Christian state be regarded. The laws of God for husbands, wives, fathers, mothers, sons, daughters, children, can not be applied, can not be obeyed, in such a community. "Husbands, love your wives," is a divine injunction. But for those most miserable outcasts of humanity, the American slaves, there can be no such law, but an admonition against it. God's claims, so expressed, interfere with man's property in man. Husbands, beware of imagining that you have any rights, any authority, in regard to the chattels you are permitted to live with; beware of ever so loving them as to be unwilling to sacrifice them at a moment's warning to the avarice, the need, or the passions of your owners. Ye are not permitted to love, but only in subjection to the price of the market, the necessities of your master, and the grand rule of your domestic institution, the slave and its increase.

Wives, be obedient to your husbands. What? Obedience from a chattel to a chattel? Wives ye are none, and this divine law belongs not to you, but for the profit of your masters. Your obedience and your increase belong to them, and to none else.

Children, obey your parents. But slaves have no children, and their children have no parents, except only as the bales of cotton have a parent in the gin and the factory, where they were shaped and bonded for the market. These commands and precepts are all and only for the masters, not the slaves. Slaves have no ties, no affections, no duties, no obligations, no belongings, but for their owners, whose property they are, and for whom and at their bidding, every faculty, capacity, emotion, must be devoted, occupied, tasked, improved, sold at the highest premium to the highest bidder whenever, however, and wherever the owner's interest requires it.

And it is not isolated beings that we devote thus, for a mere lifetime, to such degradation and cruelty, but we create a perpetual, unfailing, and self-renewing spring of this wickedness. It is not a transitory shower of blistering drops that we cause to pass over the land, but an Artesian well that we sink, of domestic shame and misery for future generations. In the word of God it is said, referring to the glory and blessedness of the establishment of righteousness and freedom as the fundamental fixtures of society: "If thou take away from the midst of thee the yoke, thou shalt raise up the foundations of many generations." But we, by foredooming unborn children to the yoke, and preparing it for them, are securing a succession of curses and crimes, crimes and curses, as the heritage of the social state. We have no more right to enact by law that the *offspring* of slaves shall be slaves, than we have to make a law that the offspring of *the free whites* shall be slaves. If such a law were passed in the State of New-York, a law that the children of those engaged in manual labor should from the birth be taken and held as chattels, to be bought and sold as the property of those capitalists for whom their parents have been laboring, could such a law sanction such a crime? Could it make it any other thing than man-stealing? Could it be pleaded that it is not man-stealing, because it is children-stealing? What is it when these children grow up?

And if they have children, does the fact that their parents were stolen before them give the stealers of the parents any claim upon the next generation? Does the fact that their parents were stolen before them take away *their* rights as human beings, and turn the stealing of them into a natural and just claim of property? Nothing can transmit the right of theft; no law can sanction it; even if we had a right to steal the parents from themselves, this could give no right to steal the children from the parents and from God. This is the deep damnation of our guilt. The offense cries up to heaven. By stealing children from the birth, we are A NATION OF MEN-STEALERS, and we renew, perpetuate and increase the guilt from generation to generation. We perpetuate the sin and the cruelty upon five times the number that our ancestors did, and insure its being perpetrated by five times more, and then thank God for the success of this providential missionary institution.

The guilt is increasing, but all the while the conscience in regard to it is diminishing and being seared. The sin, by being enlarged in surface and in quantity, seems lessened in intensity. We are more guilty than our fathers in the practice of it, and yet we contrive to make ourselves imagine that we are less guilty and more pious than they. The iniquity is a moral cancer that is eating at the vitals of our piety, while the only treatment we tolerate is increased doses of chloroform, till the whole system is stupefied under its influence. When a new outrage is committed, we just send to the apothecaries for more laudanum, or swallow, through our representatives, a Lecompton drench and sweat, or suffer Congress to administer an English swindle. Never was a sick and groaning victim more completely at the mercy of unprincipled quacks. Every six months some new experiment of fraud, despotism, bribery, unprincipled and ignorant political surgery, and we are hauled and tossed about, and cut and skinned as if we were a dead body in the dissecting-room, and Congress nothing but a class of raw, headstrong, roaring medical students with their knives in their hands and Dunglison's Anatomy in their pockets. The body does not wince, does not kick, does not even protest; and so they keep cutting and carving, no outrage as yet attempted being so monstrous as to have gone beyond the people's tame endurance.

Our iniquitous and cruel career against the African race came to its climax in the Dred Scott decision; for when iniquity takes the place of national law, and is enthroned in the tribunal of justice, it can not well go higher; and now that decision, unresisted, uncorrected, is producing its fruits. It is like the star wormwood cast upon all fountains of waters, and men drink and die. Our public officials of justice and of policy, from the highest to the lowest, every time they are about to enact a new violence against the oppressed, only have to refer to the Dred Scott decision, and the basest, meanest, most detestable acts of fraud and cruelty are converted into righteousness.

From the Secretary of State down through files of marshals, judges, bailiffs, lawyers, to the conductor of the street rail-car, the word passes, and the policy is established, and it is officially announced, and the judicial dictum is reverberated and applauded and applied, that black men have no rights that white men are bound to respect. This dictum is fast being welded into chains, into political precedents sealed and made sure, and snare after snare in the iron net is woven on by lies, by perversions of the Constitution and of history, by new measures of usurpation unresisted, by presumptuous, unauthorized interpretations of law, till the very breath of the black man is almost beaten out of his body, and he is refused the privilege of expanding his lungs in a Republican atmosphere. Our judges, Cabinet ministers, attorneys, general and local, and Secretaries of State are hunting up examples of old injustice, for precedents of new villainy. They thus set immorality and cruelty in the fountains of justice, infecting all its elements with death, just as vile assassins poison the wells of their neighbors by throwing dead dogs into them, or the carcases of cats and skunks.

As God declared in a case fearfully similar, they have turned judgment into gall and wormwood, and the fruit of righteousness into hemlock. They hunt every man his brother with a net. That they may do evil with both hands earnestly, the prince asketh, and the judge asketh for a reward; and the great man, he uttereth his mischievous desire, and so they wrap it up. The best of them is as a briar; the most upright is sharper than a thorn-hedge; they trust in vanity and speak lies; they conceive mischief and bring forth iniquity; they hatch cockatrice's eggs and weave the spider's web; he that eateth of their eggs dieth, and that which is crushed breaketh out into a viper. There is no judgment in their goings; they have made them crooked paths, speaking oppression, conceiving and uttering from the heart words of falsehood, so that judgment is turned away backward, and justice standeth afar off. They are never so happy as when they conceive absolute mischief, the dregs of profound social ignorance, prejudice, and depravity, framing mischief by a law which thenceforward they impose as the supreme political and moral state god. They set up the sin of Slavery as law, enforce it by the Constitution under judicial opinions, to which they swear allegiance, and if they can not discover precedents, they make them.

The Secretary of State dares publicly to affirm that no black man ever received a passport, and can not, as a citizen, receive one, and shall not. The Dred Scott decision has prepared this lid for the black man's living sepulchre, and Secretary Cass acts the undertaker for the body, and screws down the coffin with an incontrovertible falsehood. Then the Secretary of the Treasury declares that a free negro can not receive a register for his own vessel, nor be master of his own vessel, nor, as such, have any title to his own property by United States marine papers: for by the Dred Scott decision he is no citizen, and can be none, and to be the rightful owner and master of his own maritime property, a man must be a citizen. As he has none of the rights of a citizen, any seafaring man may own *him*, but he can not himself be the owner of so much as a plank or a nail in his own vessel. Then comes, on the heels of this outrage, the United States Land Commissioner, and from the General Land Office, with the same despotic authority under the same infernal act, declares that persons of color have no right of purchase and ownership in the public lands, that privilege also being restricted by positive law to citizens of the United States, or those that intend to become such; and by the Dred Scott decision a man with a colored skin neither is, nor can become, nor can without treason intend to become, a citizen. So, by this decision, and these magisterial interpretations and enforcements of it, the human being with a skin not colored like our own, is alienated and expelled from land and sea—is an exile every where, and even on the great highway of nations no better than a log, or a snag, or a shred of drifting sea-weed, over which the keel of a Christian civilization plunges, with all on board grinning approbation of the cruelty. And certainly, if God's word be not thundered against such crimes, the Church and the ministry do, by their silence, set the seal of a Christian approbation to all this. Our revivals of religion become accessory to it, if a fawning, cringing, whining piety, trembling in the fear of man, refuses to bear testimony against such wickedness.

And thus more and more the common heart and conscience are hardened against all remorse and repentance in such villainy, and each new administration of the slave power becomes the executor of some new and more atrocious scheme of fraud and tyranny, left in trust as a legacy by its predecessor. And men that have kept silent up to the present crisis, have had their capacity of dumbness, their grace of silence, thoroughly tried; they are indeed dumb dogs, that no provocation is likely to set to barking. If they have not yet spoken, they will forever hold their peace. What form of this wickedness can be transacted worse than the shapes in which it has already been enthroned and legalized? Would the open revival of the slave-trade be any greater atrocity than the decision that a human being with a colored skin, though born in this country, and free born, and under this Government, can not be a citizen of the United States, and has no rights that white men are bound to respect?

When this iniquity was, by this declaration and decision, publicly inaugurated in the supreme tribunal of national justice; when, in defiance of God's appointment and consecration of the judgment-seat for himself, this most astounding cruelty and robbery were proclaimed as the rule of national justice, by which men were let loose for all manner of villainy against a whole race of human beings, we imagined that the pulpit would have spoken out, if it never had before, in reprobation of an enormity in a Christian nation so atrocious, so unrivalled. The Sabbath after that prodigious judicial crime, it seemed as if the very Bibles would have burst open of their own accord, and that in living fire the lightning of God's word would almost have burned its sentence on the walls, and hissed along the congregations. We thought that even men whose lips had been sealed up to that time, would have broken that silence forever, and directed the thunders of divine truth against such fearful public enshrinement and enforcement of undissembled, undisputed inhumanity and falsehood. Instead of that, there was a tame and almost unquestioning acquiescence; and the men that did speak out, were themselves denounced as the mad accusers and revilers of God's appointed dignities. Instead of denouncing the sin, men, ministers, and editors denounced the denunciation of it as the greatest sin. It had come to pass literally, as in the fifty-ninth chapter of Isaiah, that judgment was turned away backward, and justice stood afar off, for truth was fallen in the street and equity could not enter. Yea, truth faileth, and he that departeth from evil maketh himself a prey; and the Lord saw it, and it displeased him that there was no judgment.

If ever the Church and the ministry were going to speak out, it should have been then; and if not then, I do not know that any revival of religion, on the same principles, of the same type, will produce utterance. But the calamity to a nation, when the Church and ministry are thus unfaithful to their trust, is not to be computed; nor, on the other hand, is the blessing to a nation possible to be measured, when it has a church and ministry that it can not corrupt nor silence. The Church is God's own enshrinement among a people of the living sense of right and wrong, the perception of God's claims, and the sensibility to them; and where that sensibility is vivid among the people, there is always the knowledge of their own rights and the spirit to defend them. But where that sensibility to sin, and to God's claims, dies out, where the Church does not apply God's word against sin, there both the conscience toward God and the spirit of liberty are debauched and wasted, and the nation ripens for destruction. Even the most fatal oppressions, the most vital injuries are not felt, or are submitted to with servile endurance.

Can we go any lower, any deeper, than the Dred Scott decision and its consequences? The disease having, like a run of typhus fever, reached its lowest stage, will there be a reäction of nature toward health? Is there strength enough? At this point does conscience act under the word of God? At this point is the word of God being applied? The Divine Spirit is present, as a power of individual salvation; but still, under habitual indifference, there may be a palsy of the conscience in regard to this sin. An individual was met recently by a friend, who asked him how it was with him, and he said he had been busy all winter in the revival, and was at a morning prayer-meeting every morning at six o'clock. In the course of the conversation he was asked how he felt in regard to the iniquity going on in Congress. "Oh!" said he, "I don't trouble myself about that at all; and as long as I and my family get enough to eat and to drink, Congress may do what they choose; I have no concern about it." Now of what possible avail can be whole churches of such Christians, or what effect can tuns of such piety have upon the morals of the community, or how will revivals of religion reach the sins of the nation, if piety is content with eating and drinking and attendance at six o'clock morning prayers, while the nation marches steadily to wrath and ruin?

If the Church at large are under such infatuation, then indeed the nation is ready to perish; for the Church is the salt of the earth, the conscience of the nation; and if the salt have lost its savor, wherewith shall it be salted? If the conscience of the Church is corrupted and darkened, the nation has no means of knowing its own evils, and may be far advanced toward irremediable destruction. The conscience of the Church is the only conscience that pretends to be guided by the word of God, and by that word a living conscience in the Church and ministry must be the nation's watchman.

One of the darkest and most distressing symptoms in the progress of this iniquity is the insensibility of the popular conscience under outrages that we once supposed, if ever any approximation to them were perpetrated, were even attempted, would set the nation in a blaze. Even Mr. Webster used to talk of the danger of experiments upon the conscience of the country, but we find no hazard attending them. Outrage after outrage is quietly endured, till the people become accustomed to be trampled on, and conscience utters no remonstrance. A fearful paralyzing power, a spell of stupefaction, an insensibility unto death, is on the nation; and the Church and the ministry that ought to act as the nation's conscience, are drugged and possessed with the devil of silence. So that the people are not arrested, not alarmed, not made sensible what Satan's-work is being accomplished upon them. This is a fearful treason against God and his word, a terrible betrayal of principle.

It is as if the nerves of sensation in our system refused to warn us of injury by the sense of pain, so that, as under the power of chloroform, our bodies might be hacked and maimed, and we not aware of it; as in a drunken stupor, a man might be fatally burned and not know it until too late. So, if the Church and the ministry, being God's sentinels to the nation, are bribed or drugged into silence, the nation, by such treachery, will be fatally ruined ere it is aware, and will utterly perish in its own corruption. Yet still, we talk of the world's conversion, and here in these anniversaries we drive all the multifold machinery of the societies we have set in motion, while every day our very power to manage them and to keep them from the villainy of our own example grows less, and we go boasting of our health and strength and prosperity, with this terrific disease, under which we may be staggering as a drunken man upon the very last verge of God's endurance.

The indulgence, maintenance, protection, and defense of this sin, is the one great obstacle against the missionary influence and work. It cripples us, it manacles our energies, it palsies our efforts. We are in the condition of a man whose whole left side is paralyzed, so that all the strength and life of the right side are occupied and tasked with keeping the palsied half of the body from falling. We are like a man indulging in the use of ardent spirits to a degree just bordering continually on intoxication, so that all the soberness left is but just sufficient to keep him out of the gutter. We are unfit for God's work of overcoming the idolatry of the nations, while we are in slavish subjection to the worship of this Moloch at home. And this is the upshot of all our splendid training, all our vast gifts from God, all our preparations by truth, providence, and grace, for the world's deliverance from sin and Satan! Is it such an agency, or the instrumentality of such a people, that can be relied upon for the world's conversion? Eighteen hundred years Christ crucified has been known and preached on earth, as a righteous Judge and Saviour for the poor and needy, the oppressed, and the children of the needy, and yet, in these last days, and in the nation now vaunted as the foremost Christian nation upon the face of the globe, the iniquity of Slavery itself has been revived and maintained as the missionary agency and institution of the Gospel! And all this comes from hiding instead of revealing that divine life which is the light of the world, which is the disclosure and destruction of sin, but being withheld, leaves the world in darkness, and the Church to be the nursing mother of the world's abominations. As in the absence of the solar light, there is nothing but a cellar vegetation, and the nourishing and running wild and free of monsters that shun the light and love the darkness, so in the absence or concealment of God's word, a sickly, pallid, bloodless sentimentalism of compromise and expediency takes the place of vigorous, virtuous life, and gigantic forms of iniquity breed and thrive. The tremendous despotism of Slavery is the result of the policy of silence in the churches, silence in the pulpit, silence of the ministry, the delaying and withholding of the word of God.

Where can such things end, if continued? And if the conscience of the people is not reached and roused, what hope is there that the wickedness of the Government will ever be arrested? They will go just as far as the people will let them—for their conscience is always lower and more insensible than that of the people, but never higher. The conscience of the people is the last defense of liberty—the last element of righteous power. If the conscience of the people can be set right, then there is hope in God. If they disavow and throw off this iniquity, God will not lay it to their charge; but if they do not resist it, God will certainly visit it upon them; he will let them be destroyed by it. They have sown the wind—they shall reap the whirlwind.

Here, then, are demonstrated the responsibility and duty of the Church and the ministry, as God's appointed instrumentality for training and awakening the conscience of the people. How can national sins be reached in any other way? And how in this way, except only by the Word of God, which is the sole instrument in the hands of the

Spirit of God to convince the world of sin? And how is the word of God to be applied, except by the ministry, sustained by the Church for this purpose, and on the Sabbath, when God gathers the people beneath its hearing and its power? The whole salvation of our country—the whole possibility of redemption from the sin of Slavery—rests on this question: Will the Church and the ministry be faithful? Will the ministry be faithful to God? Will the Church uphold and protect the ministry in such faithfulness? The ministry must speak out, and speak with a will, with a purpose, with a perseverance and continued pressure on the conscience.

The ministry must speak to move the country—not merely to relieve their own consciences, to clear their own skirts by a quiet declaration of opinion, or to enter a protest and then retire. The ministry can move the country, but not by resolutions in Associations or in General Assemblies, while the pulpit is as silent as the grave. There is no courage whatever, and there may be very little faithfulness, in framing resolutions which may be but an anodyne to the conscience—a dispensation from ever preaching on the subject. There are no general resolutions in the New Testament to stand in the place of pulpit faithfulness in the application of God's word; but the rule was always, and every where, to renounce the hidden things of dishonesty, not walking in craftiness, nor handling the word of God deceitfully, but by manifestation of the truth commending ourselves to every man's conscience in the sight of God. And again, we were bold in our God to speak unto you the Gospel of God with much contention, and as we were allowed of God to be put in trust with the Gospel, so we speak, not as pleasing men, but God, which trieth our hearts.

Now, the word of God is for aggression and conquests, and not a compromise, with sin. The word of God is a park of artillery—a swift-rushing mountain of thunderings and lightnings against sin, to overcome it and get it out of the world, and not a mere protest to save your own credit. The word of God is to be thundered forth by the ministry for the discomfiture of this great villainy and impiety in the judgment-seat, and in the legislature, and in the sin of man-stealing; and this is to be done in reliance upon God, and at his command, that the nation may be brought to repentance, may cry out, like any other sinners, Men and brethren, what shall we do? and may be redeemed from this mighty iniquity. It is manifest that this requires an attention to it on the part of the Church and the ministry, and a space for it in the Sabbath, and a proclamation of God's truth in regard to it, such as never has been given—never has been made. This work is yet to be done, and the power and glory of the Old Testament, the intense fires of God's love of justice, and his wrath against injustice and oppression, the forked and chain-lightnings of the prophets, and the thunderbolts of Hebrew history, are yet to be shot upon this nation's sins. Who dare do it, but a ministry commissioned of God, and illuminated and inspired by his Spirit? Who *can* do it but they only? Whose appropriate business is it to do this but theirs, and what is the duty of the Church but to support and protect them in doing this? And when and how can they do this, except on the Sabbath—their day, God's day, for instructing, reproving, and calling the world to repentance?

It is not a mincing, delicate, light notice of this iniquity that God requires, or the broad, hardened, brazen, unblushing abominations of the Government and the people demand, but a reïterated, reverberated, loud thundering of God's truth. It is very easy to say a soft, apologizing word now and then in regard to it, and excite no anger, no disturbance, and do no good, rouse no man's conscience; and not a few, in what they do say or intimate on such a subject, seem to be begging pardon of the congregation for such a painful allusion, instead of uttering God's voice fearlessly, grandly, and declaring, Thou art the man!

In this matter, Christ's dividing rule is truth—He that is not for me is against me. If men will not now speak out and act out against Slavery, their voice and influence are in favor of it. If the ministers of the Gospel, instead of the policy of silence, had poured out their vials, as God's commissioned angels, and let the thunderings, lightnings, and earthquake shake the heavens and the earth, this iniquity would long since have been arrested. It is only under the repression and enforced silence of the word of God that it has been able to advance with such giant strides, till it has taken possession of the Senatorial, Representative, Executive, and Judicial branches of our Government.

Now Satan will never cast out Satan, and this iniquity is to be staid and turned back only by the word of God and by the Church and ministry being faithful to that word. "If they had stood in my counsel," says Jehovah, "and had caused my people to hear my words, then they should have turned them from their evil way, and from the evil of their doings." Just so now. But this great and mighty result of repentance for sin is not to be got at by silence in regard to the sin: and they who keep silent in a time of temptation and trial, do, in fact, defend and daub the sin with untempered mortar. They may say that they are good Anti-Slavery men, as much opposed to this iniquity as any one; but their silence gives consent, and carries them over into the ranks of the enemy. Their pretensions of Anti-Slavery principle are, indeed, excellent, if the principle itself could be got at for use. They say it is in them, *in esse*, as the diamond is in carbon; and so, indeed, every lump of charcoal, could it speak, might say: "I am a diamond—do not treat me as if I were merely a piece of charred wood. In potential essence, the diamond is in my nature."

Ah! yes, my good friend, and, if you would only tell me how I may bring it out, and keep it in the form of diamond—how I may catch the essence, and make it stay put—you will make my fortune. But, alas! the world will never see any thing in you but charcoal! Your diamond nature does not speak out; your charcoal does.

Just so, there are many in the ministry who will be much offended if you tell them they are not opposed to Slavery—therefore, in effect, defend it. They will affirm that, in potential essence, the abhorrence of Slavery is in them, though they do not go to the extreme of ever speaking against it.

Ay, and the very difficulty is, that it never makes itself known except by a most potential silence. It is as silent and invisible as the diamond is in the charcoal, or the light in a mass of solid anthracite. On this principle there is not a dark subterranean coal mine, or bed, or pit, in existence, but what is a region of brilliant, glorious light; but, unfortunately, it needs a great many manipulations of science, a great many torturing processes of art, and operations of fire and water, to extract the material of light, and put it in shining order.

And just so with not a few, who should be lights in the ministry, but are rather like invisible, unsmelted native ores. If they might be subjected to the necessary roastings and smeltings and purifications, and the word of God extracted from them in visible, glorious form and shape, confronting and exposing the gross and damning features of this sin, then indeed it would be a powerful and conquering testimony. But what is principle good for if not to come forth in action in the time of trial, if not to withstand temptation, to rebuke iniquity, and protect the weak and down-trodden from the wicked and the strong? What is the worth of silent, inactive, concealed principle, whole acres of it, what better than treachery, or salt that has lost its savor, and is not fit even for a dunghill? What is the worth of a million candles, each hidden under its own bushel? What is the light of the Christian Church and the Christian ministry given for, but to be the light of the world? If it is hidden from the world out of fear, out of a selfish expediency, it is darkness; and if the light that is in you be darkness, how great is that darkness!

It makes us think of the recent discovery that every cubic mile of ocean contains more than two pounds weight of solid silver. How potential! It makes the mouth of a miser water; but he is forced to think: If I could only get at it! O thou mine of incalculable wealth! Two million tuns of solid silver in the Atlantic! Ye potential, silvery waves, if I could but evoke, by some concentrated, irresistible chemistry, your hidden riches!

Ay, but there's the rub. 'Tis of no more use to you than the commonest puddle of sea-water; whole leagues of it, nay, the all-surrounding ocean, at your command, of no more value than the smallest secluded nook before your own cottage on the East River. And just so, a whole cubic mile of such Anti-Slavery ministers with sealed lips, or as many as could stand together in the dry bottom of the ocean, would be of no use whatever with their principles of liberty that never speak out—their upright hearts, but silent tongues and pulpits. They are upright as the palm-tree, but they speak not; and because of their own policy of silence, they hate him that rebuketh in the gate; they are not valiant for the truth upon the earth, and, in consequence of their silence and conservative influence, the few that do speak out seem extravagant and eccentric, and are marked as madmen or fanatics; they become objects of derision, as noticeable as poor Christian and Faithful were in passing through Vanity Fair—simple, innocent creatures, who said: We buy the truth. Truth! Go to the Tract House!

But truth is not only unpopular and inexpedient on such a subject as the sin of Slavery, but exceedingly dangerous. It is not proper to be brought into the pulpit, nor mentioned on the Sabbath—that sacred day of rest, when every irritating and disturbing theme should be kept far aloof from the sanctuary and from our hearts, for we come to the Church to be comforted, and political preaching is an outrage on our feelings, and a desecration of the day of God; and preaching on the sin of Slavery is political preaching, and if you preach such preaching, it offends the pew-owners, and drives away the people from the Church, and prevents them from hiring pews, and diminishes our revenues, so that, if you preach such preaching, the best interests of the Church and society require that we should unsettle you.

Well done, Simon Magus! There you stand; unvail your face, step forth into the light; only avow that you buy your minister, and use him, or lay him on the shelf, just as you would a case of umbrellas or a bale of silk, that you settle him for pew-revenues, and that your pulpit is up at auction to the highest bidder for the man who will insure you the greatest sum total of pew-rentals, and your power is at an end. The statement of such things is enough to make them a by-word and a hissing. You never can get the people to admit that the final end of God's word is just simply to keep the finances of a society above water, or as a locomotive to drag them up-hill. God's word is given for edifying and saving souls, and not merely building temples and paying for them. And the ministers of God's word, if called to preach in Nineveh, and fleeing to Tarshish, will not much longer find the churches to be mere packet-ships, in which they can snugly sleep out the storm, and pay their passage by concealing their mission.

Concealment is not the law of God's word, but MANIFESTATION, and in times of danger and of treachery, you are compelled to vary the ordinary law of God's word, as rains and gentle showers, and to come down in a perfect cataract, as if all the windows of heaven were opened, and the fountains of the great deep broken up. We may learn something here from our colored brethren. During the war of our Revolution, it is said that at a particular important point of his lines, Washington found his sentinels, night after night, picked off by a party that could not be detected. At length he committed the care of that point to a sagacious, trusty negro, on service in the army; a negro citizen (let Secretary Cass mark it) was particularly trusted by Washington. He told him the nature of the danger, and bade him have all his wits about him, remembering the watchword, if any suspicious movement was before him, which was to call out, Who goes there? three times, and then fire. The faithful, keen-witted negro reflected and made up his mind. Past midnight his watchful ear caught the stealthy advance of the enemy, and just waiting long enough to be sure of his aim, he leveled his gun, and called out, in one sentence, at one breath, Who goes dare tree time? and then fired. The foe was shot and discovered, the alarm given, and the post saved. Sometimes we must thus concentrate, and give the warning and the shot in the same movement; not here a little and there a little, but all at once, and blow after blow followed up so rapidly, that neither compromise nor retreat shall be possible.

www.ingramcontent.com/pod-product-compliance
Lightning Source LLC
LaVergne TN
LVHW010833120826
845149LV00016B/1363